Introduction

I0406829

In the ever-evolving landscape of business, entrepreneurship stands as a beacon of innovation, resilience, and endless possibilities.

This book is a dual odyssey: the first part takes you on a rollercoaster ride through the fictional narrative of an entrepreneur's life, tracing his footsteps from the initial spark of an idea to the eventual culmination of his journey, the grand exit. This narrative, though a work of fiction, is inspired by the real-life experiences, challenges, and victories that entrepreneurs face every day. It is a tale of ambition, perseverance, and the relentless pursuit of success.

The second part of this book presents a valuable resource for aspiring and seasoned entrepreneurs alike as it provides a series of strategic business process outlines, meticulously curated to help you chart your own course in the world of entrepreneurship. Drawing from three decades of learned best practices, these outlines offer actionable insights, practical advice, and tried-and-true methodologies.

Whether you're a budding entrepreneur seeking guidance on how to get started or a seasoned business owner looking to fine-tune your strategies, this book has something to offer. By intertwining the gripping narrative of our fictional entrepreneur with the strategic insights and practical guidance of the second part of the book, the goal is to provide you with a comprehensive perspective on what it truly means to be an entrepreneur.

About the Author

RONALD C. LIPOF is a tested entrepreneurial leader and has been representing companies in a variety of industries for over three decades, moving them to the next level through merger, sale, and IPO. His expertise includes strategic planning, fine-tuning messaging, developing marketing and communications strategies, corporate and business development, negotiating strategic partnerships, and structuring merger and acquisition transactions. He received a bachelor's degree in government relations from Boston University and currently serves as a judge for the MassChallenge Start-up Accelerator. He is the author of *CANNACurious: Fundamentals of the Legal Cannabis Industry*.

ENTRANCE TO EXIT

The Entrepreneurial Path

RONALD C. LIPOF

PART 1

ENTRANCE TO EXIT
The Entrepreneurial Path

Chapter 1
The Entrepreneurial Odyssey

Unveiling the Path of Opportunity
In the heart of every dreamer lies a spark, an ember of ambition that ignites the desire to create and innovate. This journey of transformation, marked by uncertainty, courage, and unyielding determination, is the essence of entrepreneurship. Welcome to a world where ordinary individuals become architects of change, where the allure of starting a small business becomes a beacon guiding those who dare to embark on a challenging yet rewarding odyssey.

The Call of Entrepreneurship
Have you ever felt the thrill of an idea electrifying your thoughts, urging you to embark on a venture that could redefine your destiny? Have you ever said to someone "don't laugh, I have an idea". Most dismiss those thoughts, but those who act and are willing to embrace risk, take the first step towards becoming true entrepreneurs.

The Lure of Independence
One of the most magnetic aspects of entrepreneurship is the promise of independence. Most of the workforce has a set schedule, a dedicated focus, and a regular compensation rate that after forty-to-fifty hours per week, hopefully covers mandatory living and travel expenses for the household. The allure of being your own boss resonates deeply with countless individuals around the world. The prospect of breaking free from the confines of traditional employment

and embracing autonomy to steer one's own ship is a powerful draw. However, this independence comes with the weighty responsibility of nurturing an idea from infancy to maturity, of overseeing every aspect of a business's growth, and of shouldering the consequences of each decision made along the way.

The Gauntlet of Challenges and Risks

Yet, make no mistake, the path of entrepreneurship is not a stroll in the park. The journey is fraught with challenges and risks that test even the most resolute of spirits. In the early stages, entrepreneurs often find themselves navigating a labyrinth of uncertainties. The lack of a guaranteed paycheck, the constant pressure to secure funding, and the need to build a customer base from scratch. Moreover, the risk of failure looms large. A significant percentage of startups do not survive past their first few years, and the reasons are as diverse as they are numerous. Market fluctuations, changing consumer preferences, unforeseen competitors, operational hurdles, and now even economic uncertainties and global conflict can swiftly dismantle even the most promising ventures.

The Crucial Role of Perseverance and Adaptability

What ultimately distinguishes successful entrepreneurs from the rest is their ability to persevere and adapt. The journey is not a straight line; it's a roller-coaster ride with exhilarating highs and disheartening lows. Yet, those who persevere in the face of setbacks, who learn from failures and mistakes, who pivot their strategies when necessary, and who enlist seasoned advisors to help guide the ship, stand a chance to thrive even in the most turbulent waters.

A Glimpse Ahead

As we embark on this journey of exploration, our path will wind through the realms of creativity and innovation, venture capital and bootstrapping, triumphs, and tribulations. We will meet a visionary who transformed an audacious idea into a thriving empire.

So, brace yourself for a narrative that mirrors life itself; unpredictable, exhilarating, and ripe with possibilities. The entrepreneurial odyssey awaits, and the journey begins now.

Chapter 2
Conceiving the Idea

From Sparks to Stars: The Genesis of Innovation
Every remarkable journey starts with a simple or bold idea. In the world of entrepreneurship, these ideas are the seeds of innovation, the foundation upon which empires are built and destinies are shaped. But how does one stumble upon these transformative concepts? How does an ordinary individual transcend the realms of the mundane to birth an idea that could change the course of industries? Mostly by solving a problem, making a process more efficient, or enhancing the functionality and/or value of an existing product or service.

Anyone can become an Entrepreneur
Our protagonist, Alex, is a 36-year-old loan officer at a community bank. Trying to be recognized by his superiors, he is the first to arrive each morning, and the last to leave. He clocks 50-hour work weeks, not counting his 40-mile round-trip commute, and his base salary is $85,000. He is married to his junior high school sweetheart who is a real estate salesperson generating $30,000 annually. Together, they have a second grader, two leased cars, and a first mortgage. After paying all monthly bills, they are lucky to save $700.

The Birth of Imagination
Alex had always been intrigued by IoT (the Internet of Things), a technology that integrates a device with an inert object, like vehicles, electronic systems, roofs, lighting, heating systems, etc., that can measure environmental parameters, generate associated data, and transmit them through a communications network. Simply put, IoT makes things "smart" - the ability to turn your home lights on-and-off, lock and unlock doors, adjust thermostats, and start

vehicles, all remotely or automatically. Alex believed that aggregating home automation remote functionality in a single app (which did not exist at the time) would have several benefits, such as lowering utility bills, making life safer and more comfortable, and saving time and effort.

It was during a morning jog on an overcast day, that a spark of inspiration ignited within. Alex contemplated the wastefulness of leaving for work without turning down the thermostat, or wondering if he turned off the coffeemaker, or locked the doors. With every step of his early run, the concept of a smart home automation app began to take shape. How great would it be to control an entire house, lights, heat, garage door, oven, etc. from anywhere, anytime, with a simple app on a phone.

Nurturing the Seed
The initial idea was only the beginning; a seedling that required careful cultivation. Alex realized that to transform this embryonic thought into a viable business concept, research was paramount. Hours were spent poring over articles, market reports, and case studies to understand the existing landscape of smart home technology, app development, and business formation. Through this exploration, Alex gained insights into the rising demand for home automation solutions and the yet untapped potential of the intersection of the Internet and devices in homes.

Validating the Vision
An idea, however brilliant, must withstand the scrutiny of reality. Armed with newfound knowledge, Alex embarked on a journey of market validation. Interviews were conducted with potential users, industry experts, and even competitors to gauge the relevance and feasibility of the envisioned smart home automation system. These conversations not only solidified Alex's belief in the idea but

also offered invaluable feedback that refined the concept further.

From Concept to Business Model
As the idea matured, it became clear that the potential had legs. It was now time to engage legal counsel to establish the entity, and an experienced business strategist to develop initial business documentation to serve as the growth blueprints going forward.

The corporate lawyer set up the new company, filed for a Federal Employer ID Number (FEIN), drafted Articles of Incorporation, Company Bylaws, an Operating Agreement, and a Founders Agreement. The business strategist developed a comprehensive Business, Marketing and Operations Plan, created a Competitive and Risk Analysis, built a 5-year Financial Model, and developed the proposed Timeline to become operational.

The Key Takeaway: Idea Evolution
Alex's journey teaches us that a groundbreaking idea rarely emerges fully formed. It takes patience, perseverance, and an unquenchable thirst for knowledge to nurture a seed of inspiration into a thriving business concept. The journey must be thoughtful and include the external services of learned experts.

As we delve deeper into Alex's story, we'll witness how the refined concept of a smart home automation system becomes the nucleus of a business venture and explore the intricate process of turning a vision into reality, step by step, innovation by innovation.

Chapter 3
The Early Days

Navigating the Storm: Building from Scratch
The birth of a business is akin to the inception of a star – a fusion of ambition, dedication, and an unyielding drive to illuminate the universe. As we delve deeper into Alex's journey, we find ourselves in the early days of his startup, where dreams met reality, and the struggle to shape an idea into a tangible reality truly began.

The Struggles of Inception
The excitement of bringing an idea to life was palpable, but it wasn't long before the struggles set in. With $7,500 from the family's savings account, Alex took on multiple roles, morphing from visionary to marketer, coder to strategist. The days seemed endless as Alex wrestled with coding bugs, design dilemmas, and the relentless demands of building a prototype for the smart home automation system. Sleepless nights and moments of self-doubt were constant companions.

Triumphs Amidst Trials
Amidst the challenges, small triumphs began to emerge. The first successful app prototype test illuminated the room, both literally and metaphorically. This triumph fueled renewed energy, reminding Alex that each obstacle was a steppingstone toward success.

Securing the Intellectual Property
It was now time to secure the technology around the prototype to properly protect Alex's original vision that had now become operational. With an additional $6,000 loan from friends and family, the corporate lawyer filed Trademark, Copyright, and Patent Registration Applications

for a patent with the U.S. Patent and Trademark Office (USPTO) that was to be held by Alex as the inventor; and drafted and Intellectual Property (IP) and Technology Assignment Agreement so the company could appropriately use the technology.

The Quest for Funding
To transform a prototype into a market-ready product requires capital; a challenge faced by many startups. Alex embarked on the quest for funding, consulting mentors and his Board of Advisors to help navigate the territory of high-net-worth individuals, angel investors, and venture capitalists. Rejection was a recurring theme, but each "no" only fueled Alex's determination to refine the pitch and the business model. After numerous meetings and presentations, a breakthrough finally arrived in the form of a visionary, high net worth investor who saw the potential of the idea and believed in Alex's ability to execute it.

Building the Dream Team
With the new working capital hand, Alex received a fixed salary and a bonus for bringing the startup to its current level of development. Reaching this moment allowed him to leave his job at the bank, immediately repay the friends and family loan, with interest, and return the initial investment from his family's savings.

Recognizing the need for a diverse skill set and perspectives, and with new funding in hand, Alex began the process of building a team. The search was intense, involving interviews, assessments, and, most importantly, assessing cultural fit. The initial team members shared a passion for Alex's vision, a hunger for innovation, and an entrepreneurial spirit to weather the challenges that lay ahead. Once again, the corporate counsel memorialized the employment of new team members with Non-Disclosure and Employment and Independent Contractor Agreements.

Nurturing Company Culture
As the team expanded, Alex's focus shifted to establishing a company culture that mirrored the startup's values. A culture of collaboration, innovation, and open communication was cultivated. Regular brainstorming sessions, knowledge-sharing meetings, and a flexible work environment fostered an atmosphere where each team member felt empowered to contribute their unique insights.

The Takeaway: Perseverance and Teamwork
The early days of a startup are marked by both uphill battles and exhilarating victories. Alex's journey highlights the importance of perseverance in the face of adversity. The struggles, whether technical, financial, or emotional, are part and parcel of the entrepreneurial path. Moreover, the significance of a dedicated team cannot be overstated. Alex's journey from solo endeavor to a collaborative venture underscores the transformative power of a united group of individuals who share a common vision and drive.

As we continue to follow Alex's story, we will witness how the blend of ambition, teamwork, and a dash of innovation propels the startup toward its next milestones. Join us as we explore the relentless pursuit of success and the lessons learned along the way.

Chapter 4
Navigating the Challenges

Adversity as the Forge of Success
The journey of entrepreneurship is as much a tale of overcoming challenges as it is a celebration of victories. As we delve further into Alex's development efforts, we encounter a phase that tests the mettle of both the entrepreneur and the startup. Scaling a business from infancy to maturity is a tumultuous path, one that demands resilience, adaptability, and strategic finesse.

Confronting the Scaling Conundrum
With the prototype refined and the team aligned, the moment arrived to add the app to the app stores and take the leap into scaling. As the demand for the smart home automation system was growing steadily, and as Alex had secured growth capital, he streamlined operations, increased production capacity, and expanded the market presence to meet demand.

Structuring Innovative Partnerships and Alliances
Alex's creativity shone brightly as innovative partnerships were forged with local manufacturers to optimize production costs. The company's focus shifted to lean manufacturing and efficient supply chain management, allowing them to utilize its capital budgets efficiently, stretch its resources and deliver quality products to customers.

The Dance with Competition
In the realm of entrepreneurship, competition is both an adversary and an ally. New players entered the market with similar products, challenging Alex's startup to differentiate and innovate. Instead of viewing competition as a threat, Alex embraced it as a catalyst for growth. The presence of

competitors validated the market need and pushed the startup to continuously improve and evolve its offerings, maintaining its first-mover status and remaining the true leader in the rapidly evolving, yet young, category.

Sailing through Financial Storms
Financial constraints persisted as the last round of investment was consumed. Balancing the need for investment in research and development with the need for short-term revenue generation required a delicate balance. Alex explored a mix of funding sources, from reinvesting profits to securing additional rounds of investment. Each financial decision was made with an eye on both short-term survival and long-term sustainability. Fortunately, the previous investor was pleased with the startup's growth and provided a follow-on round of financing to support customer acquisition and marketing initiatives.

Customer Acquisition: The Lifeline
A business's existence hinges on its ability to attract and retain customers. Alex's startup embarked on a customer acquisition journey that aggressively blended online marketing, social media engagement, and personalized outreach. Through effective storytelling, highlighting the impact of their product on everyday life, the startup began to resonate with a broader audience.

The Lesson: Turning Hurdles into Steppingstones
Alex's story teaches us that challenges are not roadblocks but opportunities for growth. Resource constraints can foster creative problem-solving, competition can drive innovation, and financial limitations can encourage strategic decision-making. In the face of adversity, it is the entrepreneur's ability to adapt, learn, and pivot that ultimately defines the trajectory of the business.

As we journey further into the heart of Alex's startup venture, we will witness how these challenges and their subsequent solutions contribute to shaping a resilient, adaptable, and forward-thinking business. Join us as we unravel the next chapters of triumphs, setbacks, and the ongoing pursuit of success.

Chapter 5
Gaining Traction

Rising from the Shadows: The Dawn of Recognition
In the tumultuous landscape of entrepreneurship, moments of recognition are like rays of sunlight breaking through the clouds. As we continue to follow Alex's journey, we enter a phase where the small business begins to gain traction, slowly emerging from obscurity into the spotlight. It's a chapter of transformation, marked by strategic decisions, customer engagement, and a commitment to continuous improvement.

The Spark of Recognition
After countless hours of hard work, strategic planning, and resourceful problem-solving, the smart home automation app began to garner attention. Reviews from early adopters started trickling in, praising the app's functionality and ease of use. These early sparks of recognition validated the startup's mission and signaled the potential for wider acceptance.

Listening to Customer Feedback
One of the crucial drivers of success during this phase was the startup's commitment to customer-centricity. Alex and the team actively sought feedback from users, engaging in open dialogues to understand pain points, suggestions, and ideas for improvement. This feedback loop led to iterative product enhancements that better aligned with customer needs and preferences.

Fine-Tuning Marketing Strategies
Recognition may spark interest, but effective marketing is the fuel that propels a business forward. Alex's startup embraced a multi-faceted marketing approach. They utilized

social media platforms to engage with a broader audience, sharing success stories and educational content about the benefits of home automation. Influencer partnerships, workshops, and webinars were organized to showcase the value of the smart home automation app in real-world scenarios.

Expanding Market Presence
As the positive reviews and effective marketing efforts combined, the startup's market presence expanded. Word-of-mouth recommendations and referrals played a significant role in this growth. This momentum allowed the startup to explore new markets and regions, further diversifying its customer portfolio.

Strategic Alliances and Collaborations
Recognizing the power of collaboration, the startup formed strategic alliances with complementary businesses. Partnerships were forged with appliance companies, architects, and homebuilders, allowing the smart home app to be seamlessly integrated into new and existing buildings. These collaborations not only expanded the startup's reach but also positioned it as an industry leader.

The Takeaway: From Recognition to Sustainability
Alex's journey through the phase of gaining traction underscores the importance of a customer-centric approach, continuous improvement, and strategic marketing. By listening to customer feedback, refining the product, and effectively communicating its value, the startup was able to transform recognition into sustainable growth.

As we continue into the narrative, we invite you to join us as we explore the transformative power of customer engagement and strategic partnerships in shaping the trajectory of a business.

Chapter 6
From Emerging to Established

An Unstoppable Ascent: Beyond Startup Status
The path from startup to established business is a journey of evolution, marked by key milestones that reflect growth, adaptability, and resilience. In this chapter, we witness how Alex's small business navigated the transition from emerging player to an established entity, conquering new horizons and facing the complexities that come with growth.

Crossing the Threshold: Growth Milestones
The startup's journey continued with a series of pivotal milestones that shaped its trajectory. The first major milestone was the acquisition of its Series A round, its first significant round of venture capital financing. This influx of capital empowered the business to continue to scale its operations, accelerate product development, and expand its market presence. With the product's functionality and reliability firmly established, the startup entered strategic partnerships to market the smart app with large retailers and homebuilders. This move amplified the product's accessibility, making it available to a wider audience and driving sales to new heights.

Expansion into New Markets
As the startup gained traction, it also gained the confidence to explore new markets and verticals. International markets beckoned, and through a series of licensing relationships, the smart home automation system soon found its place in homes across different countries. This expansion required cultural sensitivity, regulatory adaptation, and localization of marketing strategies, which the company adeptly navigated.

Challenges of Maintaining Company Values
With growth, the challenge of maintaining the core values that defined the startup's identity became increasingly pronounced. Alex recognized that as the team grew and the business expanded, it was imperative to uphold the commitment to innovation and customer-centricity that had propelled them to success. This required fostering a strong company culture, embedding values into decision-making processes, and ensuring that every team member was aligned with the overarching mission.

The Tug of War: Scaling and Integrity
As the business expanded, the tension between scaling and preserving integrity emerged. The startup faced decisions that pitted rapid growth against the risk of diluting the original vision. Each new market, each partnership, demanded a careful balance between seizing opportunities and staying true to the values that originally defined the business's identity.

Building a Legacy
Despite the challenges, the journey from emerging startup to an established entity was a testament to the startup's ability to evolve while staying rooted in its founding principles. The passion for innovation and the dedication to customer satisfaction remained at the heart of every decision made, solidifying the business's place as a respected industry player.

The Lesson: Anchoring Growth in Values
Alex's journey exemplifies that the transformation from emerging startup to established business hinges on the ability to navigate the delicate dance between growth and values. By expanding into new markets, forging strategic partnerships, and maintaining a steadfast commitment to

core principles, the business not only thrived but also established itself as a force to be reckoned with.

As we move deeper into the narrative, we'll explore how the business's established status opens new avenues for innovation, collaboration, and impact. Join us in witnessing the unfolding chapters of success, challenges, and the enduring pursuit of a meaningful legacy.

Chapter 7
Embracing Change

The Art of Adaptation: Thriving Amidst Transformation
In the dynamic landscape of business, change is the only constant. As we journey further into Alex's narrative, we find ourselves in a chapter that explores the small business's ability to not only weather change but also to thrive by embracing it. This is a tale of innovation, agility, and the art of continuous improvement in maintaining a competitive edge.

Winds of Change: Industry Shifts
The startup's journey unfolded against the backdrop of an evolving industry. Technological advancements, regulatory changes, and shifts in consumer preferences created ripples that resonated throughout the business landscape. Rather than resisting these shifts, the small business saw them as opportunities to redefine its offerings.

Adapting to Consumer Demands
Consumer preferences are the compass that guides businesses. Recognizing this, Alex's company keenly listened to feedback, monitored market trends, and conducted thorough consumer research. This agility allowed them to pivot their product offerings in response to changing demands. New features were added, existing ones were refined, and the product line expanded to cater to a broader spectrum of needs.

Innovation as a Driver of Success
Innovation is the cornerstone of longevity in any industry. The small business, having established itself as a pioneer, continued to push the boundaries of what was possible. A dedicated research and development team was formed to

explore emerging technologies and trends. This commitment to innovation birthed novel features, enhancements, and even entirely new products that further cemented the business's reputation as an industry leader.

The Role of Continuous Improvement
In the face of change, continuous improvement became a mantra. The company's culture of innovation permeated every aspect of its operations, from production processes to customer service. Regular assessments, feedback loops, and data analysis drove ongoing refinement. The business was in a state of constant iteration, with each cycle honing its offerings to better match consumer needs.

Staying Competitive through Agility
The key to the business's sustained competitiveness lay in its agility. By recognizing change as an opportunity rather than a threat, the company stayed ahead of the curve. Strategic alliances with technology partners, cross-industry collaborations, and quick adaptation to market shifts positioned the business as a beacon of adaptability.

The Lesson: The Power of Adaptation
Alex's journey through the chapter of embracing change underscores the importance of staying malleable in the face of shifting tides. By actively seeking opportunities for innovation, remaining receptive to consumer feedback, and fostering a culture of continuous improvement, the business not only navigated change but thrived within it.

As we advance forward in the story, we will witness how this agility and innovation propels the small business toward greater heights. Join us as we explore the ways in which adaptation and evolution become the driving forces behind a resilient, dynamic, and future-ready enterprise.

Chapter 8
The Peak and Plateau

Navigating the Landscape of Success and Stagnation
The entrepreneurial journey is a landscape of undulating terrain marked by exhilarating peaks and challenging plateaus. In this chapter, we delve into the phases of peak achievement and subsequent plateau, witnessing how Alex's small business grappled with the emotional and strategic complexities that arise during these distinct phases of its trajectory.

Reaching the Summit: Peak Achievement
After years of perseverance, innovation, and strategic decision-making, the small business reached a peak of success. Market share expanded, revenues surged, and the product gained widespread recognition. This phase was a culmination of hard work, and the team basked in the glow of well-deserved triumph.   Yet, even at the summit, challenges persisted. The pressure to maintain the momentum and continually meet high expectations became a constant companion. The business had to not only deliver on existing promises but also chart a path to sustain this growth and prevent stagnation.

The Plateau's Deceptive Stillness
As the initial euphoria waned, a sense of plateau settled in. The growth curve that had previously been steep began to level off. The business, having conquered so much, now faced a new challenge: maintaining relevance and staying dynamic in the face of familiarity. The plateau was a testing ground for both the entrepreneur's resilience and the business's adaptability. It required innovative thinking, the courage to revisit strategies, and a willingness to disrupt even when things seemed stable.

Strategic Pivots and Emotional Resilience
The plateau posed not only strategic but also emotional challenges. For Alex and the team, it was a period of reflection and recalibration. The elation of success was replaced by a yearning for the next milestone. The entrepreneur's emotional resilience was put to the test, as the plateau cast shadows of doubt and stagnation. Strategically, the business needed to reevaluate its value proposition, explore new markets, or, once again, innovate product offerings.

Renewed Innovation: Overcoming the Plateau
Innovation emerged as the catalyst to overcome the plateau. By reimagining the business's offerings, identifying unmet needs, and exploring adjacent markets, the business found a path to reignite growth. The company's commitment to constant improvement and adaptability was instrumental in shattering the stagnation and setting the stage for a new phase of ascent.

The Lesson: Peaks as Springboards and Plateaus
Alex's journey through the peak and plateau phase underscores that success is not a destination but a journey. Peaks offer a moment of celebration and achievement, but they should also be seen as springboards for even greater aspirations. Plateaus, though challenging, can be catalysts for innovation and change, pushing a business to redefine its boundaries and embrace new frontiers.

As we continue to explore Alex's journey, we will witness how the business begins to think about exiting.

Chapter 9
Deciding the Exit

Farewell to Familiar Shores: Navigating the Exit
Every entrepreneurial journey, no matter how extraordinary, reaches a crossroads where the decision to exit becomes an inevitable reality. In this chapter, we delve into the profound moments that led Alex to consider departing from the venture that was once just a spark of imagination. We explore the diverse exit options available, each with its own implications and possibilities.

The Reflection of Change
As the small business's journey progressed, Alex and the team found themselves in a moment of reflection. The company that had been nurtured from an embryonic idea had grown into a mature, successful entity. While the journey had been exhilarating, the time had come to weigh the scales of passion and practicality. Alex's own aspirations, the evolving industry landscape, and personal circumstances all played a role in prompting the decision to consider an exit.

Understanding Exit Options
An exit is not a singular path but a spectrum of choices, each with its own set of implications and benefits. Alex faced a trio of primary exit options: acquisition, Initial Public Offering (IPO), and handing over the reins.

1. Acquisition: Passing the Torch
The acquisition option involved selling the business to a larger company that recognized the value it had created. While this could provide financial rewards, it also meant ceding control and seeing the business integrated into a larger entity.

2. IPO: Going Public

An IPO would open the doors to the public market, allowing the business to raise capital by selling shares to investors. While this option could bring substantial funds and visibility, it would also introduce new regulatory complexities and demands from shareholders.

3. Handing Over the Reins: Legacy Building

Choosing to hand over the reins to a capable successor was another path. This would allow the business's legacy to continue while freeing Alex to pursue new endeavors. It would, however, require careful selection of the right successor and a comprehensive transition plan.

Balancing Emotional and Practical Factors

The decision to exit was not solely driven by financial considerations. Emotional ties to the business, its team, and the values it stood for were also influential factors. Alex's journey was marked by moments of introspection, seeking counsel from mentors, and aligning personal aspirations with the broader strategic direction.

The Lesson: The Essence of Transition

Alex's journey through the exit decision highlights the essence of transition in entrepreneurship. The decision to exit is not a defeat, but a culmination of growth and evolution. It's a choice made at the crossroads of personal aspirations, business reality, and industry trends.

As we step deeper into the unfolding narrative, we will witness how Alex navigates the complexities of the exit decision and how it shapes the legacy of the business. Join us in exploring the emotional and strategic intricacies of bidding farewell to a venture that was once a dream transformed into reality.

Chapter 10
Preparing for the Exit

Crafting the Epilogue: Navigating the Transition
As the decision to exit crystallizes, a new chapter begins; one that involves meticulous preparation to ensure a smooth transition and to maximize the value of the business. In this chapter, we delve into the intricate process of preparing for the exit, addressing the legal, financial, and operational considerations that define this crucial phase.

The Prelude to Transition
Alex decided to sell the company to a competitor, creating the single largest market share in the smart home automation sector. With the decision to exit made, Alex's focus shifted to orchestrating a seamless transition. A series of steps needed to be taken to optimize the business's value, maintain its integrity, and facilitate the shift of ownership.

Financial Optimization
Maximizing the business's value required a thorough financial assessment. A seasoned accounting firm was hired, and the books were meticulously reviewed to ensure they were in order and that potential acquirers or investors would find the financial records transparent and appealing. Any lingering operational inefficiencies were addressed, and opportunities to bolster revenues or cut costs were explored. Strategic advisors were brought on to help identify areas to enhance operational efficiencies.

Operational Streamlining
Operational efficiency was of paramount importance. Processes were streamlined to ensure they were well-documented, easily transferable, and capable of maintaining the same level of quality and reliability under new

ownership. This not only instilled confidence in the potential buyer but also ensured a smooth transition period.

Legal Considerations
Legal intricacies needed careful attention to avoid any surprises during the exit process. Intellectual property rights, contracts, licenses, and any ongoing legal disputes were meticulously reviewed. Legal experts were engaged to ensure all legal documents were in order, minimizing potential obstacles that could arise during negotiations, and the Definitive Membership Interest Purchase Agreement was drafted.

Team Communication and Transition
The team was a vital element in the transition process. Open communication with employees about the impending exit was crucial to maintain morale and retain valuable talent. A clear transition plan was developed to ensure continuity and provide reassurance to the team that their roles and contributions would still be valued under the new ownership. Alex would be retained for 90 days as a transition advisor.

The Lesson: The Symphony of Preparation
Alex's journey through the phase of preparing for the exit underscores the importance of meticulous preparation and negotiation. The transition from ownership to new ownership demands a harmonious blend of financial optimization, operational streamlining, legal diligence, and team communication.

As we journey through the final chapters of this narrative, we will witness how careful preparation leads to a seamless transition and a legacy that endures even as ownership changes hands. Join us in exploring the final stages of Alex's entrepreneurial voyage that encompasses both the culmination of one chapter and the opening of another.

Chapter 11
The Exit Strategy

Sealing the Fate: Navigating the Transition
The culmination of an entrepreneurial journey lies in the execution of the chosen exit strategy. In this chapter, we delve into the intricate process of negotiating and executing the exit strategy, as well as exploring the emotional impact that the transition has on the founder and the dedicated team that has journeyed alongside them.

Negotiating the Deal
As the chosen exit strategy unfolded, the negotiation table became a stage for careful deliberation. Alex's strategic acumen came to the forefront as he and his strategic advisors navigated the terms of the acquisition, balancing financial considerations with the preservation of the business's legacy and values. The negotiations were a dance of compromise, ensuring a fair deal that recognized the business's worthwhile aligning with Alex's aspirations.

The Buyer and the company mutually agreed upon a Purchase Price as a 5x multiple of EBITDA (Earnings Before Interest, Taxes, Depreciation, and Amortization). They debated the tax consequences of an Asset vs Membership Interest purchase structure. They negotiated the amount of cash at closing and the term of the balance of the Purchase Price in a Seller Note with an agreed upon interest rate, and they set escrow parameters and a closing date.

Execution of the Exit
With the deal terms finalized, the execution of the exit began. Legal documents were signed, approvals were obtained, and the transition of ownership commenced. This phase involved meticulous attention to detail, ensuring that every facet of

the business's operation was seamlessly handed over to new leadership.

Embracing Change: Emotional Impact
While the exit represented a strategic decision, it was also a profoundly emotional journey for Alex and the dedicated team that had been integral to the business's success. As the day of transition approached, a mixture of emotions flooded in; pride for what had been accomplished, anticipation for new beginnings, and a touch of nostalgia for the journey that had led to this point.

Managing the Team's Transition
The transition also posed unique challenges for the team. Uncertainty about the future, concerns about changes in company culture, and the emotional ties forged over the years all added complexity to the process. Open communication, transparency about the transition, and reassurances from leadership played a pivotal role in helping the team navigate the change.

The Legacy Lives On
The execution of the exit strategy marked the closing of one chapter and the opening of another. While Alex bid farewell to the business they had nurtured, the legacy of innovation, sustainability, and customer-centricity endured. The business was poised to embark on a new trajectory under new leadership, but the impact it had made under Alex's guidance remained a testament to their entrepreneurial journey.

Financially, after sharing the exit proceeds with the company's high net worth investor, and the Series A funding partner, Alex received a reward capable of providing generational wealth.

The Lesson: The Balance of Strategy and Emotion
Alex's journey through the execution of the exit strategy showcases the intricate interplay between strategic decision-making and emotional connection. The exit is not only about financial transactions but also about the preservation of legacy, values, and the well-being of the team that contributed to the business's success.

As we delve deeper into the final chapters of this narrative, we will witness how the exit strategy marks a transformative turning point that allows both the founder and the business to embark on new adventures while cherishing the imprint left behind. Join us in exploring the culmination of Alex's journey and the dawn of a new era.

Chapter 12
Reflection and Legacy

Echoes of the Journey: Lessons and Legacy
The journey of an entrepreneurial venture, from its inception to its exit, is an odyssey marked by discovery, transformation, and growth. In these final chapters, we take a moment to reflect on the path that Alex's small business traversed, the lessons learned, the legacy established, and the impact made on an entire industry.

Celebrate the Successes
The journey was a mosaic of triumphs, both small and monumental. From the first prototype that illuminated a room to the strategic partnerships that expanded the business's reach, each success was a testament to vision, determination, and collaboration. These moments of celebration, born from tireless effort and unwavering commitment, form the foundation of the business's narrative.

Triumph Over Challenges
No journey is devoid of challenges, and Alex's was no exception. The struggles faced, be it financial constraints, fierce competition, or the emotional toll of decision-making, were not roadblocks, but rather steppingstones. The journey showcases the power of perseverance and the potential of the human spirit to rise above adversity, emerging stronger and more resilient.

The Legacy That Endures
As the entrepreneurial voyage reaches its conclusion, the legacy left behind shines brightly. The small business's impact on innovation and customer empowerment leaves an indelible mark. The products developed, the partnerships forged, and the team's dedication serve as a testament to the

business's role in shaping the industry and leaving a lasting imprint.

Beyond the Horizon
The end of one journey is merely the beginning of another. As Alex steps away from the venture that was once a seedling of an idea, new possibilities await. The lessons learned, the experiences gained, and the network built throughout this journey become valuable assets to carry forward into new endeavors. The entrepreneurial spirit, ignited and nurtured, continues to blaze on.

The Final Lesson: The Unfinished Symphony
Alex's journey from humble beginnings to a transformative exit underscores that entrepreneurship is not a destination but an ever-evolving expedition. The final chapter serves as an invitation for others to embark on their own odysseys, inspired by the story of innovation, resilience, and the power to create change.

As we conclude this narrative, we invite you to take these lessons and reflections into your own pursuits, crafting your own narratives of growth, impact, and legacy. Join us in celebrating the journey of entrepreneurship that never truly ends, but rather transforms into the symphony of the future.

Chapter 13
Conclusion

Lessons for Aspiring Entrepreneurs
The journey of Alex's small business has been a symphony of innovation, challenges, growth, and transformation. As we draw the curtain on this narrative, let's reflect on the key takeaways and insights that offer guidance to those who dare to embark on their own entrepreneurial odyssey.

1. Vision is Your North Star
Your journey begins with a vision. Let it guide your decisions, inspire your actions, and fuel your persistence. Your vision is the foundation upon which you'll build your business and leave your mark on the world. The phrase "don't laugh, I have an idea" could lead to greatness.

2. Resilience in the Face of Adversity
Challenges are not setbacks but steppingstones to growth. Embrace them with resilience, tenacity, and an unwavering belief in your ability to overcome obstacles. The journey demands perseverance in the face of adversity.

3. Innovation is a Lifeline
Innovation is the heartbeat of entrepreneurship. Continuously seek opportunities to innovate, evolve, and stay ahead of the curve. Embrace change and use it as a catalyst for growth.

4. Customer-Centricity is Paramount
Your customers are the lifeblood of your business. Listen to their feedback, understand their needs, and build solutions that truly address their pain points. A customer-centric approach is the foundation of sustainable success.

5. Adapt to Thrive

The business landscape is ever-changing. Embrace change as an opportunity for growth. Adaptation is the key to maintaining relevance and remaining agile in the face of shifting tides.

6. Collaborate for Impact

Partnerships and collaborations are the seeds of exponential growth. Forge alliances that amplify your reach, broaden your perspective, and create opportunities for shared success. Engage legal, strategic, and financial advisors to help guide the way and provide best practices.

7. Embrace Risk with Wisdom

Entrepreneurship is inherently risky, but calculated risks can yield remarkable rewards. Be bold in your decisions, but also thoughtful and strategic in your approach to risk-taking.

8. Legacy is a Continuous Journey

A legacy isn't built overnight; it's woven through every decision, interaction, and innovation. Strive to leave behind a legacy that reflects your values, your impact, and your dedication to creating positive change.

9. It's About the Journey, Not Just the Destination

Remember that entrepreneurship is not solely about reaching a destination; it's about the journey itself. Celebrate both successes and setbacks, as each contributes to your growth as an entrepreneur.

10. Your Story Awaits

As you embark on your own entrepreneurial journey, remember that your story is unique and valuable. Embrace challenges as opportunities, celebrate every milestone, and above all, believe in your ability to make a difference.

In Closing: The Symphony Continues
The journey of entrepreneurship is a harmony of ambition, creativity, and resilience. As the curtain falls on this narrative, it rises on yours. Take the lessons learned, the wisdom gained, and the spirit of innovation as your guiding lights. Your story is waiting to be written, your legacy waiting to be forged.

With unwavering determination, courage, and a commitment to excellence, you are poised to craft your own narrative of success. The ensemble of entrepreneurship continues, and the world awaits the harmony you'll create.

Epilogue

The Echoes of Triumph: A Legacy Continues
As we conclude this narrative, let us take a glimpse into the post-exit chapter of Alex's entrepreneurial journey. The impact of the small business's success reverberates not only in financial gains, but in the legacy it leaves behind. A legacy that continues to shape the industry and inspire future generations of entrepreneurs.

With this final note, we celebrate the legacy of Alex's small business, the impact it made on the industry, and the spirit of entrepreneurship that continues to shape the world. As the pages of this story close, new stories of innovation and legacy are waiting to be written. New dreamers begin their journey on the entrepreneurial path, working diligently to, one day, achieve their exit on the horizon.

KEY STARTUP SUMMARIES

"How-To" Overviews

Strategic and business planning documentation which serves as a roadmap to provide direction to the business and is often required to obtain financing.

PART 2

Table of Contents

Business Plan Table of Contents

A comprehensive business plan typically includes various sections that cover every aspect of the business.

Here's a table of contents for a comprehensive business plan:

Table of Contents

1. **Executive Summary**
   - Business Description
   - Mission Statement
   - Summary of Key Highlights
   - Funding Requirements

2. **Business Description**
   - Company Name and Structure
   - Legal Structure and Ownership
   - History and Background
   - Vision and Mission Statements
   - Core Values

3. **Market Analysis**
   - Industry Overview
   - Market Size and Growth Trends
   - Target Market Segmentation
   - Customer Profiles
   - Competitive Analysis
   - SWOT Analysis

4. **Products or Services**
   - Product/Service Description
   - Unique Selling Proposition (USP)
   - Development Stage

- Intellectual Property
- Research and Development

5. **Marketing and Sales Strategy**
   - Marketing Objectives and Goals
   - Market Entry and Expansion Strategy
   - Pricing Strategy
   - Promotion and Advertising
   - Sales Channels
   - Sales Forecast

6. **Operational Plan**
   - Location and Facilities
   - Equipment and Technology
   - Supply Chain Management
   - Production or Service Delivery Process
   - Quality Control
   - Inventory Management

7. **Management and Team**
   - Management Team Profiles
   - Organizational Structure
   - Roles and Responsibilities
   - Advisors and Consultants
   - Hiring Plan

8. **Financial Plan**
   - Financial Projections (Income Statement, Cash Flow Statement, Balance Sheet)
   - Break-Even Analysis
   - Funding Requirements
   - Sources of Funding
   - Use of Funds
   - Exit Strategy (if applicable)

9. **Risk Analysis and Mitigation**
    - Identification of Business Risks
    - Risk Assessment and Probability
    - Mitigation Strategies
    - Contingency Plans

10. **Legal and Regulatory Compliance**
    - Business Licenses and Permits
    - Intellectual Property Protection
    - Contracts and Agreements
    - Compliance with Industry Regulations

11. **Implementation Timeline**
    - Milestones and Timetables
    - Critical Path Analysis
    - Gantt Chart

12. **Marketing Plan**
    - Marketing Goals and Objectives
    - Marketing Tactics and Activities
    - Marketing Budget
    - Marketing Metrics and Key Performance Indicators (KPIs)

13. **Sales Plan**
    - Sales Goals and Objectives
    - Sales Strategies and Tactics
    - Sales Team Structure
    - Sales Training and Development

14. **Monitoring and Measurement**
    - Key Performance Indicators (KPIs)
    - Milestone Tracking
    - Financial Performance Monitoring
    - Market Research and Feedback Loops

15. **Appendices**
- Additional Supporting Documents (e.g., resumes of key team members, product images, market research data, legal agreements, etc.)

16. **References**
- Citations and References for Data and Information Used in the Plan

This comprehensive business plan provides a structured and detailed overview of your business concept, strategy, and operations, making it a valuable tool for attracting investors, securing financing, and guiding your business's growth and development.

Market Entry and Expansion Strategy Plan

Creating a Market Entry and Expansion Strategy plan for a startup is essential for charting a successful path into new markets and ensuring sustainable growth.

Here's a comprehensive plan tailored to a startup:

Executive Summary

- Provide a brief overview of your startup's status and the objective of entering or expanding in the target market.
- Highlight the key benefits and growth potential of this market entry/expansion.

Market Analysis

1. Market Research

- Describe the target market, including its size, growth trends, and relevant demographics.
- Identify emerging trends, customer needs, and market gaps.

2. Competitive Analysis

- Analyze your competitors in the target market, highlighting their strengths, weaknesses, and market share.
- Assess entry barriers and key success factors.

Entry/Expansion Strategy

3. Market Entry Mode

- Determine the most appropriate entry mode (e.g., direct sales, partnerships, e-commerce, etc.) based on market conditions and startup resources.

4. Market Segmentation and Targeting

- Define the specific market segments your startup aims to target.
- Explain why these segments were chosen and how your startup will address their unique needs.

5. Product/Service Adaptation

- Detail how your startup's products/services will be adapted to suit local market preferences and comply with regulations.

6. Pricing Strategy

- Develop a pricing strategy that considers local pricing norms, competitor pricing, and any discounts or promotions.

Marketing and Sales Strategy

7. Marketing Plan

- Outline the marketing channels and tactics to reach your target audience (e.g., digital marketing, content marketing, social media).
- Include a budget and timeline for marketing activities.

8. Sales Plan

- Describe your sales approach, including distribution channels, sales team structure, and sales targets.
- Define metrics to measure sales effectiveness.

Operations and Logistics

9. Supply Chain and Distribution

- Explain how products/services will be sourced, manufactured (if applicable), and distributed within the target market.
- Address logistics challenges and potential solutions.

10. Regulatory and Compliance

- Identify and outline the regulatory requirements in the target market, and detail how your startup plans to comply with them.

Financial Projections

11. Budget and Financial Forecast

- Provide a detailed budget that encompasses market entry/expansion costs, including initial investment and ongoing operational expenses.
- Forecast revenue and profit projections for the first few years in the target market.

12. Risk Assessment

- Identify potential risks and challenges associated with market entry/expansion.
- Develop strategies to mitigate and manage risks.

Implementation Timeline

13. Project Timeline

- Create a comprehensive timeline with key milestones for the market entry/expansion process.
- Assign responsibilities and set deadlines.

Monitoring and Evaluation

14. Key Performance Indicators (KPIs)

- Define KPIs to measure the success of your market entry/expansion.
- Establish a regular reporting and review process to assess progress.

Conclusion

- Summarize the critical points of the plan.
- Reiterate your startup's commitment to entering or expanding successfully in the target market.

Appendices

- Include any supplementary materials, such as market research reports, legal documents, or market-entry checklists.

Keep in mind that this Market Entry and Expansion Strategy plan should serve as a dynamic roadmap that adapts as market conditions change and your startup gains more insights. Regularly review and adjust your strategies based on real-world feedback and results and be open to seeking expert advice when entering new markets to maximize your chances of success.

Marketing Metrics and Key Performance Indicators

Here's a list of marketing metrics and key performance indicators (KPIs) that are important for a small business:

1. **Website Traffic Metrics:**
   - Website Visitors
   - Page Views
   - Bounce Rate
   - Average Session Duration

2. **Conversion Metrics:**
   - Conversion Rate
   - Cost Per Conversion
   - Sales Revenue
   - Lead Generation

3. **Email Marketing Metrics:**
   - Open Rate
   - Click-Through Rate (CTR)
   - Conversion Rate from Emails
   - Unsubscribe Rate

4. **Social Media Metrics:**
   - Follower Growth
   - Engagement Rate
   - Reach and Impressions
   - Social Media Shares

5. **Content Marketing Metrics:**
   - Blog Post Views
   - Time on Page
   - Content Downloads
   - Social Shares of Content

6. **Paid Advertising Metrics:**
   - Click-Through Rate (CTR)
   - Cost Per Click (CPC)
   - Cost Per Mille (CPM)
   - Return on Ad Spend (ROAS)

7. **Search Engine Optimization (SEO) Metrics:**
   - Organic Traffic
   - Keyword Ranking
   - Backlinks
   - Organic Conversion Rate

8. **Customer Acquisition and Retention Metrics:**
   - Customer Acquisition Cost (CAC)
   - Customer Lifetime Value (CLTV)
   - Churn Rate
   - Repeat Purchase Rate

9. **Customer Engagement Metrics:**
   - Customer Satisfaction (CSAT)
   - Net Promoter Score (NPS)
   - Customer Feedback and Reviews
   - Customer Retention Rate

10. **Marketing ROI Metrics:**
    - Return on Investment (ROI)
    - Marketing Cost as a Percentage of Revenue
    - Customer Acquisition ROI
    - Marketing Channel ROI

11. **Mobile App Metrics (if applicable):**
    - App Downloads
    - In-App Engagement
    - App Store Ratings and Reviews
    - User Retention Rate

12. **Competitor Metrics:**
   - Market Share
   - Competitor Keyword Ranking
   - Competitor Social Media Metrics

13. **Lead Generation Metrics:**
   - Lead Generation Rate
   - Cost Per Lead
   - Lead-to-Customer Conversion Rate

14. **Content Engagement Metrics:**
   - Video Views
   - Time Watched (for videos)
   - eBook or Whitepaper Downloads
   - Comments and Feedback on Content

15. **Local Business Metrics** (if applicable)**:**
   - Local SEO Performance
   - Local Listings Accuracy
   - Customer Reviews on Local Platforms

Remember that the specific metrics and KPIs you track may vary depending on your business goals, industry, and marketing channels. It's essential to regularly analyze these metrics to make data-driven decisions and improve your marketing efforts.

Due Diligence Overview

During the due diligence process of buying or selling a company, various business documents and records are typically requested to assess the company's financial health, legal compliance, operations, and overall value.

Here's a comprehensive list of documents often required:

1. **Financial Documents:**

   - **Financial Statements:** Balance sheets, income statements, and cash flow statements for the last 3-5 years.
   - **Tax Returns:** Corporate tax returns and any relevant personal tax returns of key executives or owners.
   - **Budgets and Projections:** Current and future financial forecasts and budgets.
   - **Audit Reports:** Any external audit reports or internal audit findings.
   - **Accounts Receivable and Payable:** Detailed lists of outstanding invoices and debts.
   - **Bank Statements:** Statements from all business bank accounts.

2. **Legal Documents:**

   - **Articles of Incorporation/Formation:** The company's official formation documents.
   - **Bylaws/Operating Agreement:** Internal governance documents.
   - **Contracts and Agreements:** All contracts with customers, suppliers, employees, and other parties.

- **Intellectual Property:** Documentation related to patents, trademarks, copyrights, and licenses.
- **Litigation History:** Records of past or pending lawsuits, disputes, or investigations.
- **Regulatory Compliance:** Documents related to industry-specific regulations and permits.
- **Insurance Policies:** Copies of insurance policies, including liability, property, and key person insurance.

3. **Operational Documents:**

- **Inventory Records:** Detailed inventory lists and valuation.
- **Asset List:** A list of all tangible and intangible assets owned by the company.
- **Leases and Real Estate:** Property and equipment leases, deeds, and related documents.
- **Employee Records:** Employment agreements, organizational charts, and benefit plans.
- **Supplier and Customer Lists:** Lists of major suppliers and customers.
- **Business Plan:** Current and historical business plans and strategies.

4. **Tax Documents:**

- **Sales Tax Records:** Records of sales tax collection and remittance.
- **Tax Compliance:** Documentation of compliance with federal, state, and local tax laws.
- **Tax Credits and Incentives:** Any applicable tax credits or incentives received.

5. **Environmental and Regulatory Documents:**

- **Environmental Reports:** Environmental assessments, permits, and compliance records.
- **Occupational Safety:** Occupational health and safety records and compliance documentation.

6. **Employee and HR Documents:**

- **Employee Benefits:** Benefit plans, retirement plans, and employee policies.
- **Payroll Records:** Payroll tax records, wage information, and employment contracts.
- **Employee Handbooks:** Company policies and procedures.

7. **Intellectual Property and Technology:**

- **Technology Agreements:** Software licenses, IT contracts, and technology agreements.
- **Intellectual Property Ownership:** Documentation of IP ownership and usage rights.

8. **Market and Competitive Analysis:**

- **Market Research:** Market analysis reports, customer surveys, and competitive intelligence.

9. **Customer and Supplier Contracts:**

- **Customer Agreements:** Major customer contracts, including terms and commitments.
- **Supplier Agreements:** Agreements with key suppliers, including pricing and terms.

10. Insurance Policies:

- **Liability and Business Insurance:** Policies covering various aspects of the business.

11. Due Diligence Reports:

- **Previous Due Diligence Reports:** If available, previous due diligence reports.

12. Financial Projections:

- **Future Financial Projections:** Long-term financial forecasts and growth plans.

13. Corporate Governance:

- **Board Meeting Minutes:** Minutes from board meetings and other governance documents.

This list is not exhaustive, as the specific documents required may vary depending on the nature of the business, industry, and the buyer's preferences. It's crucial to work with legal and financial professionals experienced in mergers and acquisitions to ensure a thorough and accurate due diligence process.

Startup and Growth Investors

When seeking investment for a business or startup, you can explore various sources of funding, including friends and family, high net worth individuals, financial institutions, and different rounds of venture capital funding (Series A, Series B, and Series C).

Here's a list of possible investors from each category:

1. **Friends and Family:**
   - Close friends who believe in your business ideas.
   - Family members are willing to invest in your venture.
   - Personal contacts who have expressed interest in supporting you.

2. **High Net Worth Individuals (HNIs) and Angel Investors:**

   - Wealthy individuals who invest in startups and early-stage businesses.
   - Angel investor networks or groups.
   - Entrepreneurs who have successfully exited their own businesses.

3. **Financial Institutions:**

   - Banks: Traditional bank loans or lines of credit.
   - Credit Unions: Member-owned financial cooperatives.
   - Online Lenders: Platforms offering various loan products.

4. **Venture Capital (VC) Firms:**

- **Series A Round:** Typically, the first institutional funding round.
  - o Venture capital firms specializing in early-stage investments.
  - o Corporate venture arms of larger companies.

- **Series B Round:** For scaling and expanding operations.
  - o VCs with a focus on growth-stage companies.
  - o Private equity firms interested in growth-stage investments.

- **Series C Round:** Geared toward further scaling and market expansion.
  - o Late-stage VC firms.
  - o Institutional investors looking for established startups.

5. **Private Equity Firms:**

- Private equity firms with a focus on mature businesses seeking growth or restructuring.

6. **Corporate Investors:**

- Established companies looking to invest in startups for strategic reasons.
- Companies seeking to acquire startups as part of their growth strategy.

7. **Crowdfunding Platforms:**

   - Crowdfunding websites where individuals can contribute small amounts of money.
   - Equity crowdfunding platforms allow investors to purchase equity in startups.

8. **Government Grants and Programs:**

   - Government agencies offer grants or low-interest loans to businesses.
   - Incubators and accelerators affiliated with government initiatives.

9. **Strategic Partners:**

   - Companies in a related industry can provide not only capital but also strategic support and access to their network.

10. **Venture Debt Providers:**

    - Lenders offer debt financing to startups, often alongside equity investments.

11. **Institutional Investors:**

    - Pension funds and endowments seeking diversified investment opportunities.

12. **Corporate Venture Capital (CVC):**

    - Corporate divisions or subsidiaries dedicated to investing in startups aligned with their business interests.

13. **Family Offices:**

- Private wealth management firms that manage investments for high-net-worth families.

14. **Foundations and Nonprofits:**

- Organizations with a mission to support entrepreneurship and innovation.

15. **Accelerators and Incubators:**

- Programs providing seed funding, mentorship, and resources in exchange for equity.

16. **Strategic Alliances:**

- Partnerships with other businesses that can provide financial support.

17. **Supplier or Customer Financing:**

- Negotiating favorable payment terms with suppliers or customers to free up capital.

When seeking investment, it's crucial to match your funding needs, growth stage, and business model with the most appropriate sources of capital. Each type of investor has its own expectations, requirements, and risk tolerance, so understanding your target investors and crafting a compelling pitch is essential for success.

M&A Transaction Structures

Merger and acquisition (M&A) transactions can take various structures, depending on the specific goals and circumstances of the parties involved. Here's a list of common M&A structures:

1. **Asset Purchase:**

   - Acquirer purchases specific assets and liabilities of the target company.
   - Allows the acquirer to choose which assets and liabilities to assume.
   - Common in situations where the target company has significant liabilities or where the buyer wants to cherry-pick assets.

2. **Stock Purchase (Share Purchase or Equity Purchase):**

   - The acquirer buys the ownership (equity or shares) of the target company.
   - The acquirer assumes both the assets and liabilities of the target.
   - Often used when the buyer wants to acquire the entire business with its existing structure and contracts.

3. **Membership Interest Purchase (LLC Purchase):**

   - Like a stock purchase but used for limited liability companies (LLCs).
   - The buyer acquires membership interests in the LLC.

- All assets and liabilities of the LLC typically transfer to the buyer.

4. **Merger (Amalgamation):**

- The target company is merged into the acquirer, resulting in a single surviving entity.
- Can be structured as a "forward merger" (target merges into the acquirer) or a "reverse merger" (acquirer merges into the target).
- Requires shareholder approval in many cases.

5. **Joint Venture:**

- Two or more companies form a new entity to pursue a specific business opportunity or project.
- Parties often contribute assets, capital, or expertise to the joint venture.
- Can be structured as a separate legal entity (e.g., a corporation or LLC) or a contractual arrangement.

6. **Spin-Off (Divestiture):**

- A company separates one of its divisions or subsidiaries into a standalone entity.
- The newly formed entity can be sold, taken public, or operated independently.

7. **Tender Offer:**

- The acquirer makes a public offer to purchase a significant number of shares directly from the target company's shareholders.
- Often used in hostile takeovers or when the buyer wants to acquire a substantial ownership stake.

8. **Asset Swap:**

- Two companies exchange assets or business units.
- Typically used when the assets being exchanged have similar values or strategic importance.

9. **Stock Swap (Equity Swap):**

- The acquirer offers its own shares in exchange for the target company's shares.
- Shareholders of the target become shareholders of the acquirer.

10. **Leveraged Buyout (LBO):**

- Typically used in private equity acquisitions.
- The acquirer uses a significant amount of debt financing to purchase the target company, often with the target's assets serving as collateral.

11. **Reverse Takeover (RTO):**

- A private company acquires a public company to gain access to public markets and become a publicly traded entity.

12. **Management (MBO) & Employee (EBO) Buyouts:**

- MBO - A company's existing management team, often with the support of external investors, buys the company from its current owners.
- EBO – A transaction where the employees purchase a business from its owner.

13. **Distressed Sale:**

- Occurs when a financially troubled company is sold, often through bankruptcy proceedings or out-of-court restructuring.

The choice of M&A structure depends on various factors, including the strategic goals of the parties, tax implications, regulatory requirements, and the financial health of the target and acquirer. Legal and financial advisors play a crucial role in determining the most appropriate structure for a specific M&A transaction.

What to Include in an Investor Presentation

An investor presentation is a critical tool for pitching your business to potential investors, whether you're seeking venture capital, angel investors, or other sources of funding. It should be clear, concise, and compelling.

Here's a list of what to include in an investor presentation:

1. Cover Slide:
- Company name and logo.
- Presentation title.
- Presenter's name and title.
- Date of the presentation.

2. Executive Summary:
- A brief overview of your business, its purpose, and the investment opportunity.
- Key highlights and value proposition.

3. Problem Statement:
- Clearly define the problem or market need your business addresses.
- Explain the pain points or challenges faced by potential customers.

4. Solution:
- Describe your product or service and how it solves the identified problem.
- Highlight the unique features and benefits of your solution.

5. Market Opportunity:
- Present the market size, growth potential, and target audience.

- Provide data and statistics to support your claims.

6. Business Model:
- Explain how your business generates revenue.
- Outline pricing strategies, sales channels, and distribution methods.

7. Traction and Milestones:
- Showcase key achievements, milestones reached, and customer or user adoption.
- Highlight any partnerships or notable contracts.

8. Competitive Landscape:
- Identify competitors and their strengths and weaknesses.
- Explain how your business differentiates itself.

9. Marketing and Sales Strategy:
- Outline your marketing and customer acquisition strategies.
- Describe your sales process and channels.

10. Financial Projections: Present financial forecasts, including income statements, cash flow projections, and balance sheets. - Discuss assumptions and growth rates. Show key financial metrics.

11. Funding Needs: Specify the amount of funding you are seeking. - Explain how the funds will be used (e.g., product development, marketing, expansion). - Discuss the desired terms of the investment.

12. Team: Introduce the key members of your team, their roles, and their relevant experience. Highlight any advisors or mentors.

13. Use of Funds: Provide a breakdown of how the invested capital will be allocated. Explain how it will support business growth and development.

14. Risk Analysis: Identify potential risks and challenges your business may face. Explain your mitigation strategies.

15. Exit Strategy: Discuss potential exit scenarios for investors, such as acquisition or initial public offering (IPO).

16. Ask for Investment: Clearly state what you are asking from the investors. Specify the type of investment (equity, convertible note, etc.).

17. Appendix: Include any additional supporting documents, charts, graphs, or data that enhance your presentation. This could include customer testimonials, market research, or legal agreements.

18. Q&A Session: Allocate time at the end of the presentation for questions and answers.

Remember to keep the presentation concise and engaging. Use visuals and graphics to support your points and make the content easy to digest. Practice your delivery to ensure that you can effectively convey your message and respond to investor inquiries. Tailor your presentation to your audience and their specific interests and expectations.

Startup Documents Overview

Starting a business involves a variety of legal, financial, and operational tasks, and you'll need several documents to ensure that you are compliant with local regulations and that your business operates smoothly. The specific documents required can vary depending on your business structure, location, and industry.

Here's a list of common documents you may need to start a business:

1. Business Plan:

- A comprehensive business plan outlining your business concept, target market, competition, marketing strategy, and financial projections.

2. Business Name Registration:

- Proof of business name registration, often done with the appropriate government agency.

3. Business Structure Documentation:

- **For sole proprietorships and partnerships**: Registration of the business name and any partnership agreements.
- **For LLCs** (Limited Liability Companies): Articles of Organization or Certificate of Formation.
- **For corporations**: Articles of Incorporation.

4. Employer Identification Number (EIN):

- A federal tax ID number issued by the IRS for tax purposes.

5. Business License and Permits:

- Local, state, and federal business licenses and permits are required for your specific industry and location.

6. Business Bank Account Documentation:

- Proof of opening a separate business bank account, which is essential for keeping business finances separate from personal finances.

7. Operating Agreement or Bylaws:

- For LLCs and corporations, documents outlining the management and operating structure of the business.

8. Trademarks and Intellectual Property Documents:

- If applicable, documents related to trademarks, patents, copyrights, or trade secrets.

9. Contracts and Agreements:

- Contracts for services, partnerships, or leases.
- Employment contracts when hiring employees.

10. Insurance Policies: Business insurance policies, such as liability insurance, property insurance, key person, or workers' compensation.

11. Financial Records: A chart of accounts, accounting software, and records of initial capital investment. A business budget and financial projections.

12. Tax Documents: Documentation related to federal, state, and local tax registration and compliance.

13. Location Lease or Property Documentation: If you're leasing a physical location, your lease agreement. Property deeds or titles if you own the property.

14. Employee Records: - Employee handbooks, job descriptions, and any required HR documentation.

15. Health and Safety Permits: - Permits related to health and safety regulations, particularly if you're in the food service or healthcare industry.

16. Environmental Permits: - Environmental permits if your business operations have an environmental impact.

17. Import/Export Documentation: - If applicable, documentation for international trade, including import/export licenses.

18. Industry-Specific Licenses and Certifications: - Any licenses or certifications required for your specific industry, such as a real estate license or medical license.

19. Website and Online Presence Documentation: - Domain registration, terms of use, privacy policy, and any e-commerce agreements for online businesses.

Remember that the specific documents you need can vary depending on your location and the nature of your business.

Valuing a Small Business

Valuing a small business is a complex process that involves assessing various factors and financial metrics. There isn't a one-size-fits-all methodology because the approach can vary depending on the nature of the business, its industry, and the specific circumstances of the sale.

Here is a general methodology commonly used to value small businesses:

1. **Gather Financial Information:**

   - Start by collecting comprehensive financial statements and records for the business. This includes income statements, balance sheets, cash flow statements, and tax returns for the past 3-5 years.
   - Normalize the financials by adjusting for any one-time or non-recurring expenses or revenues. This helps create a more accurate picture of the business's ongoing operations.

2. **Select a Valuation Approach:**

   - There are several approaches to valuing a small business, including the Asset Approach, Income Approach, and Market Approach. Depending on the business type and industry, one or more of these approaches may be appropriate.

3. **Asset Approach:**

   - This approach focuses on the business's assets and liabilities.

- Calculate the net asset value (NAV) by subtracting the total liabilities from the total assets.
- Suitable for businesses with significant tangible assets like real estate or equipment.

4. **Income Approach:**

- This approach assesses the business's ability to generate future cash flows.
- The most common method within the Income Approach is the Discounted Cash Flow (DCF) analysis.
- Estimate future cash flows the business is expected to generate, apply a discount rate (reflecting the risk associated with the investment), and calculate the present value of those cash flows.
- The DCF method often provides a comprehensive and forward-looking valuation.

5. **Market Approach:**

- This approach compares the small business to similar businesses that have been sold recently.
- Look at market multiples (price-to-earnings ratios, price-to-sales ratios, etc.) of comparable businesses in the same industry.
- Apply the multiples to the financial metrics of the small business to estimate its value.
- This approach is valuable when there is a robust market for comparable businesses.

6. **Weighted Average Approach:**

- In many cases, it's wise to consider multiple valuation methods and assign weights to each based on their relevance and reliability.
- For example, you might give a higher weight to the DCF method but also consider the Market Approach to cross-verify the results.

7. **Consider Non-Financial Factors:**

- Financial metrics alone don't capture the full value of a small business. Consider non-financial factors like the competitive landscape, industry trends, customer relationships, and the strength of the management team.

8. **Calculate the Final Valuation:**

- After applying the chosen methods and considering all relevant factors, arrive at a range of values.
- The final valuation is often determined through negotiation between the buyer and seller, considering the specific circumstances of the sale.

9. **Engage Professional Help:**

- Valuing a small business can be challenging, and it's advisable to engage the services of a professional business appraiser or financial advisor experienced in small business valuations.
- Legal and accounting experts can also provide valuable guidance in the process.

10. Continuous Monitoring and Updates:

- Business valuations may change over time due to shifts in the market, business performance, or external factors. It's essential to periodically reassess the value, especially if you are planning to sell or seek investment.

Remember that small business valuation is both an art and a science. It often involves subjective judgments and negotiation. The methodology should be tailored to the specific circumstances and objectives of the valuation.

What to Include in a Financial Proforma

A financial proforma, also known as a financial projection or forecast, is a forward-looking financial statement that estimates a company's future financial performance. It typically includes a comprehensive set of financial projections, assumptions, and key performance indicators to help assess the financial health and potential of a business.

A confidential disclosure should be included indicating that the information provided is forward-looking, based on the opinions and estimates of the company, and has been prepared for discussion purposes only.

Here's a list of what is typically included in a financial proforma:

1. **Income Statement (Profit and Loss Statement):**

   - Revenue or Sales Forecast: Projections of future sales or revenue streams.
   - Cost of Goods Sold (COGS): Estimates of direct costs associated with producing goods/services.
   - Gross Profit: Revenue minus COGS.
   - Operating Expenses: Forecasts of general and administrative expenses, marketing expenses, and other operating costs.
   - Operating Income (or Loss): Gross profit minus operating expenses.
   - Interest Expenses: Projections of interest paid on loans or debt.
   - Other Income and Expenses: Forecasts of miscellaneous income and expenses.
   - Net Income (or Loss): The bottom-line profit or loss.

2. **Cash Flow Statement:**

- Operating Cash Flow: Projections of cash generated from daily operations.
- Investing Cash Flow: Forecasts of cash flows related to investments in assets (e.g., equipment, property).
- Financing Cash Flow: Projections of cash flows related to financing activities (e.g., loans, equity investments).
- Net Cash Flow: The change in cash for a specific period.

3. **Balance Sheet:**

- Assets: Projections of what the company owns, including cash, accounts receivable, inventory, and fixed assets.
- Liabilities: Projections of what the company owes, such as accounts payable, loans, and other debts.
- Equity: Projections of the owner's equity or shareholder equity.
- Total Assets, Liabilities, and Equity: The fundamental accounting equation: Assets = Liabilities + Equity.

4. **Revenue Breakdown:**

- A breakdown of revenue by product or service categories, customer segments, geographic regions, etc.

5. **Expense Breakdown:**

- A detailed breakdown of operating expenses, including salaries, rent, utilities, marketing costs, and others.

6. **Assumptions:**

- A clear list of assumptions used in building the proforma, such as growth rates, pricing changes, and expense increases.

7. **Key Performance Indicators (KPIs):**

- Metrics and ratios that provide insights into the company's performance, such as gross margin, net profit margin, return on investment (ROI), and break-even point.

8. **Sensitivity Analysis:**

- Scenarios that explore the potential impact of different assumptions and external factors on financial projections. This helps assess the robustness of the proforma.

9. **Break-Even Analysis:**

- Calculations to determine the level of sales needed to cover all expenses and reach a break-even point.

10. **Capital Expenditure (CapEx) Projections:**

- Forecasts of investments in capital assets, including equipment, property, and technology.

11. Working Capital Analysis:

- Projections of current assets and liabilities to assess liquidity and short-term financial health.

12. Debt Schedule:

- If applicable, a schedule of principal and interest payments on outstanding loans.

13. Investment Analysis:

- Metrics like return on investment (ROI), payback period, and net present value (NPV) for assessing the viability of projects or investments.

14. Funding Requirements:

- Identification of any external funding needed to support the business's growth or operations.

15. Financial Ratios:

- Key financial ratios, such as the current ratio, quick ratio, and debt-to-equity ratio, provide insights into the company's financial health.

It's important to note that the financial proforma should be based on realistic and well-documented assumptions. Additionally, it should be periodically updated and revised to reflect changing business conditions and goals. Financial projections are a valuable tool for planning and decision-making in a business, but their accuracy depends on the quality of the underlying assumptions and data.

A Startup SWOT Analysis

Here is a SWOT analysis for a hypothetical startup company:

Strengths:

1. **Innovative Product**: ABC Startup has developed a groundbreaking product that addresses a critical need in the market.

2. **Talented Team**: The company is comprised of a highly skilled and motivated team with expertise in technology and industry-specific knowledge.

3. **Strategic Partnerships**: ABC Startup has established partnerships with key players in the industry, providing access to resources, distribution channels, and industry insights.

4. **Agile and Adaptable**: The startup is nimble and can quickly respond to market changes and adapt its product offerings accordingly.

5. **Cost-Efficiency**: The company operates with a lean structure, minimizing overhead costs and maximizing resource allocation.

Weaknesses:

1. **Limited Market Awareness**: Being a startup, ABC Startup may struggle with low brand recognition and limited market awareness, making it challenging to attract early customers.

2. **Funding Constraints**: As a new entrant, the company may face difficulties in securing adequate funding for scaling operations and marketing efforts.

3. **Product Development Risks**: There may be uncertainties related to the development and scalability of the innovative product, which could lead to delays or technical challenges.

4. **Competition**: The industry is saturated with established competitors, which may make it difficult for the startup to gain market share.

5. **Dependency on Key Personnel**: The loss of key team members could significantly impact the company's ability to execute its business plan.

Opportunities:

1. **Growing Market**: The industry segment in which ABC Startup operates is experiencing rapid growth, driven by increasing demand for its solutions.

2. **Market Niche**: The startup can carve out a niche market by focusing on unique features or customer segments that competitors have overlooked.

3. **International Expansion**: There's an opportunity to expand globally as the product gains traction in the domestic market.

4. **Technological Advancements**: Leveraging emerging technologies such as AI, IoT, or blockchain can enhance the company's product offerings and market positioning.

5. **Strategic Alliances**: Forming alliances with complementary businesses can open new distribution channels and customer bases.

Threats:

1. **Market Competition**: Established competitors with larger budgets and market presence may aggressively target ABC Startup's market share.

2. **Regulatory Changes**: Changes in regulations and compliance requirements could create challenges or increase operating costs.

3. **Economic Downturn**: Economic recessions or downturns may lead to reduced customer spending on technology solutions.

4. **Intellectual Property Theft**: Protecting intellectual property and technology from theft or infringement is a constant concern.

5. **Cybersecurity Risks**: With increasing reliance on technology, the company faces the constant threat of cybersecurity breaches, potentially damaging its reputation and customer trust.

This SWOT analysis provides an overview of the startup's internal strengths and weaknesses and external opportunities and threats. It can serve as a valuable tool for strategic planning and decision-making to capitalize on strengths, mitigate weaknesses, pursue opportunities, and address threats effectively.

Startup Benchmark and Milestone Plan

A Benchmark and Milestone Plan is a critical tool for tracking progress and ensuring that a project or startup is meeting its objectives at key points in its development.

Below is an example of a Benchmark and Milestone Plan for a software development startup:

Month 1-2: Project Initiation and Planning
- Benchmark 1: Define project scope, goals, and objectives.
- Milestone 1: Complete project charter and secure necessary resources.
- Milestone 2: Assemble project team and assign roles and responsibilities.

Month 3-4: Market Research and Analysis
- Benchmark 2: Conduct thorough market research and competitor analysis.
- Milestone 3: Compile market research findings and identify target customer segments.
- Milestone 4: Define unique selling points (USPs) for the product.

Month 5-6: Product Design and Development
- Benchmark 3: Create a detailed product design and development plan.
- Milestone 5: Complete product prototype and conduct initial testing.
- Milestone 6: Incorporate feedback and refine the product design.

Month 7-8: Alpha Testing and Feedback
- Benchmark 4: Begin alpha testing with an internal testing team.
- Milestone 7: Identify and address major bugs and issues.
- Milestone 8: Collect feedback from alpha testers and make necessary improvements.

Month 9-10: Beta Testing and User Acceptance
- Benchmark 5: Launch beta version for a select group of external users.
- Milestone 9: Monitor beta testing for user experience and performance.
- Milestone 10: Gather user feedback and prioritize final adjustments.

Month 11: Final Testing and Quality Assurance
- Benchmark 6: Complete final product testing and quality assurance.
- Milestone 11: Ensure the product meets all performance and security standards.

Month 12: Product Launch and Marketing
- Benchmark 7: Prepare for product launch, including marketing and promotion.
- Milestone 12: Officially launch the product in the market.
- Milestone 13: Monitor initial market reception and collect user feedback.
- Milestone 14: Begin post-launch marketing and customer support.

Ongoing: Post-Launch Evaluation and Growth
- Benchmark 8: Continuously monitor user engagement, sales, and customer feedback.

- Milestone 15: Identify areas for improvement and plan for updates and enhancements.
- Milestone 16: Develop a strategy for scaling the product and expanding the customer base.

This Benchmark and Milestone Plan provides a structured timeline with clear objectives, benchmarks, and milestones at each stage of the project's development. It helps the team stay on track, measure progress, and make informed decisions to ensure the successful development and launch of the product. It's important to note that this plan can be customized based on the specific needs and complexity of the project or startup.

Risk Analysis

Risk analysis is a crucial component of a startup's strategic planning. It helps identify potential risks and uncertainties that the company may face and develop strategies to mitigate or manage them effectively.

Here is a risk analysis for a hypothetical startup company:

Market Risks:

1. **Market Saturation:** The market for the startup's product may already be saturated with established competitors, making it challenging to gain market share.

   Mitigation: Conduct thorough market research to identify gaps or niches in the market. Focus on unique selling points and differentiation strategies.

2. **Economic Downturn:** Economic recessions or downturns could reduce customer spending on technology solutions, impacting the startup's revenue.

   Mitigation: Diversify revenue streams and maintain a financial buffer to weather economic uncertainties.

Product Development Risks:

3. **Technical Challenges:** Developing an innovative product may encounter unforeseen technical challenges, leading to delays or cost overruns.

Mitigation: Maintain a skilled and adaptable development team, conduct rigorous testing, and have contingency plans for potential setbacks.

4. **Intellectual Property Theft:** Protecting the startup's intellectual property from theft or infringement is crucial to maintain a competitive edge.

   Mitigation: Invest in robust intellectual property protection, including patents, trademarks, and trade secrets. Implement security measures to safeguard proprietary information.

Operational Risks:

5. **Funding Constraints:** Securing adequate funding for startup operations, marketing, and growth may be challenging.

   Mitigation: Develop a comprehensive business plan, explore multiple funding sources (e.g., venture capital, angel investors, grants), and maintain a lean operating structure.

6. **Dependency on Key Personnel:** The loss of key team members could significantly impact the company's ability to execute its business plan.

   Mitigation: Cross-train team members, establish clear knowledge transfer protocols, and consider succession planning.

Regulatory and Compliance Risks:

7. **Regulatory Changes:** Changes in regulations and compliance requirements could create challenges or increase operating costs.

   Mitigation: Stay informed about industry regulations, maintain compliance, and adapt quickly to changes with a legal and regulatory team.

Cybersecurity Risks:

8. **Data Breaches:** With increasing reliance on technology, the startup faces the constant threat of cybersecurity breaches, potentially damaging its reputation and customer trust.

   Mitigation: Invest in robust cybersecurity measures, conduct regular security audits, and train employees on best practices.

Market Adoption Risks:

9. **Limited Market Awareness:** As a startup, the company may struggle with low brand recognition and limited market awareness.

   Mitigation: Develop a strong marketing and branding strategy, including targeted advertising and public relations efforts.

10. **Competitive Pressure:** Established competitors may try to imitate or outperform the startup's product.

Mitigation: Continuously innovate, enhance the product, and focus on building strong customer relationships.

Financial Risks:

11. **Cash Flow Challenges:** Poor financial management or unexpected expenses could lead to cash flow problems.

    Mitigation: Maintain a meticulous financial plan, track expenses rigorously, and consider securing a line of credit for emergencies.

Environmental Risks:

12. **Natural Disasters:** Environmental factors like hurricanes, earthquakes, or floods could disrupt operations.

    Mitigation: Implement disaster recovery and business continuity plans to ensure minimal disruption during such events and maintain proper insurance.

Regularly reviewing and updating this risk analysis is essential for a startup to adapt to changing circumstances and ensure its long-term success. It also helps in making informed decisions about risk acceptance, risk transfer, or risk mitigation strategies.

Competitive Analysis

A competitive analysis is a critical component of a startup's strategic planning process. It helps the company understand its competitive landscape, identify strengths and weaknesses relative to competitors, and develop strategies to gain a competitive edge.

Below is an example of a competitive analysis for a hypothetical startup company (ABC Startup) operating in the technology sector:

1. Competitor Identification:

- **Competitor A (Market Leader):** Established in 2005, Competitor A is the current market leader with a wide range of products and a strong customer base.
- **Competitor B (Niche Player):** Competitor B specializes in a specific niche within the technology sector and has a loyal customer following.
- **Competitor C (Emerging Startup):** Competitor C is a recently established startup with a focus on innovative solutions but limited market presence.

2. Product and Service Comparison:

- **ABC Startup:** Offers a unique, cutting-edge technology product that addresses a specific industry pain point.
- **Competitor A:** Provides a comprehensive suite of products but lacks the specialized focus of ABC Startup.
- **Competitor B:** Specializes in a niche area but lacks the breadth of offerings.

- **Competitor C:** Offers innovative solutions but is relatively untested in the market.

3. Market Share and Positioning:

- **ABC Startup:** Currently holds a small market share but is gaining attention due to its innovation.
- **Competitor A:** Dominates the market with a substantial share and widespread recognition.
- **Competitor B:** Holds a modest market share in its niche segment.
- **Competitor C:** Is still working on establishing a market foothold.

4. Pricing Strategy:

- **ABC Startup:** Offers competitive pricing for its unique product, aiming to attract early adopters.
- **Competitor A:** Typically has higher prices due to its established reputation.
- **Competitor B:** Prices its niche products at a premium.
- **Competitor C:** Uses competitive pricing to gain market entry.

5. Marketing and Branding:

- **ABC Startup:** Actively invests in marketing and branding efforts to increase visibility and awareness.
- **Competitor A:** Has a well-established brand with a broad marketing presence.
- **Competitor B:** Focuses on niche marketing strategies.
- **Competitor C:** Invests in online marketing and social media to build awareness.

6. Strengths and Weaknesses:

- **ABC Startup:**
  - Strengths: Innovation, agility, unique product.
  - Weaknesses: Limited market share, less brand recognition.
- **Competitor A:**
  - Strengths: Established market presence, diverse product range.
  - Weaknesses: Slow to adapt to market changes, potentially higher prices.
- **Competitor B:**
  - Strengths: Niche expertise, loyal customer base.
  - Weaknesses: Limited product range, small market share.
- **Competitor C:**
  - Strengths: Innovation, competitive pricing.
  - Weaknesses: Limited market presence, unproven track record.

7. Opportunities and Threats:

- **Opportunities:**
  - Growing demand for innovative solutions.
  - Partnerships and collaborations with industry leaders.
  - Expansion into untapped geographic markets.
  - Ancillary products.

- **Threats:**
  - Intense competition from established players.

- Rapid technological advancements requiring constant innovation.
- An economic downturn that affects customer budgets.
- Competitor's access to greater capital.

8. Competitive Strategy:

- **ABC Startup:** Focus on continuous innovation, targeted marketing, and strategic partnerships to gain market share gradually.

This competitive analysis provides a comprehensive overview of ABC Startup's competitive landscape, helping the startup identify areas of opportunity, threats to navigate, and strategies to pursue to thrive in the technology sector. It should be regularly updated to reflect changes in the competitive environment and inform the startup's decision-making process.

Integration Plan Following Acquisition

Creating a comprehensive integration plan is crucial when following an acquisition. This plan should outline the steps, timelines, responsibilities, and strategies to ensure a smooth transition and maximize the value of the acquired company.

Here's a sample integration plan:

1. Define Objectives and Goals:
- Clearly state the strategic objectives of the acquisition.
- Set specific, measurable, achievable, relevant, and time-bound (SMART) integration goals.

2. Integration Leadership:
- Appoint an Integration Team Leader responsible for overseeing the entire process.
- Establish cross-functional integration teams with representatives from both companies.

3. Communication Strategy:
- Develop a comprehensive communication plan for employees, customers, vendors, and other stakeholders.
- Ensure transparency and consistency in all communication efforts.

4. Cultural Integration:
- Assess the cultures of both companies to identify similarities and differences.
- Develop strategies to merge cultures while preserving core values.

5. Legal and Regulatory Compliance:
- Review all contracts, agreements, and legal obligations of both companies.
- Ensure compliance with all relevant laws and regulations.

6. IT and Systems Integration:
- Evaluate IT systems, infrastructure, and data compatibility.
- Plan for data migration, system integration, and potential upgrades.
- Ensure cybersecurity measures are in place to protect sensitive information.

7. HR and Talent Integration:
- Review the organizational structure, job roles, and compensation packages.
- Develop a plan for staff retention, training, and, if necessary, downsizing.
- Address any legal or compliance issues related to employment.

8. Customer Integration:
- Assess customer bases, identify overlaps, and create a strategy for customer retention.
- Communicate changes and benefits to customers to maintain their trust.

9. Supplier and Vendor Integration:
- Review supplier and vendor relationships and contracts.
- Identify opportunities for cost savings or optimization.
- Integrate outsourced relationship unless redundant.

10. Financial Integration:
- Merge financial systems, accounting practices, and reporting mechanisms.
- Align budgeting and financial planning processes.

11. Product and Service Integration:
- Evaluate the product or service portfolios of both companies.
- Determine how to integrate, rebrand, or phase out products or services as needed.

12. Sales and Marketing Strategy:
- Develop a unified sales and marketing strategy to cross-sell and upsell products or services.
- Ensure consistent messaging and branding.

13. Risk Management:
- Identify potential risks and develop risk mitigation plans.
- Continuously monitor and adjust strategies as needed.

14. Timeline and Milestones:
- Create a detailed integration timeline with specific milestones.
- Regularly track progress and adjust as necessary.

15. Employee Training and Support:
- Provide training and support to employees to help them adapt to changes.
- Address concerns and provide opportunities for career development.

16. Performance Metrics:
- Establish Key Performance Indicators (KPIs) to measure the success of the integration efforts.
- Monitor and report on progress regularly to stakeholders.

17. Post-Integration Evaluation:
- Conduct a thorough evaluation of the integration process.
- Identify lessons learned and areas for improvement.

18. Continuous Improvement:
- Maintain a culture of continuous improvement, where feedback is valued and acted upon.

A well-structured integration plan helps manage the complexities of merging two companies and sets the stage for long-term success. It's essential to involve key stakeholders, maintain open communication, and adapt the plan as necessary to ensure a seamless transition.

Collaboration

In the rapidly evolving landscape of technology and human collaboration, we find ourselves at an unprecedented crossroads. The convergence of artificial intelligence and human ingenuity has birthed a new era of possibilities, reshaping the way we create, learn, and connect. It is within this extraordinary juncture that this literary creation, one that exemplifies the synergy between thirty years of human learning and intellect and artificial intelligence, was developed.

"Entrance to Exit [The Entrepreneurial Path]" is a testament to the power of collaboration across dimensions. This book is a true alliance of human creativity and the capabilities of ChatGPT, an advanced AI language model developed by OpenAI. Through a process of iterative ideation, thoughtful analysis, and genuine dialogue, the words you just read emerged as a harmonious duet between a human author and artificial intelligence.

The journey that led to the creation of this book began with the author leveraging more than three decades of learned experiences and business best practices with the extensive reservoir of information and linguistic dexterity provided by ChatGPT. The result is a testament to the potential of AI-augmented human expression that truly transcends the limitations of individual perspectives.

www.ingramcontent.com/pod-product-compliance
Lightning Source LLC
Chambersburg PA
CBHW072334290526
45794CB00002B/866